6512

1

Iron Harp

for Pat
let the white birds sing
the sea change

Thomas.
E.
Kinsella

Works by Thomas Fitzsimmons

Planet Forces
Fencing the Sky
The Dream Machine
Rune of Stone
Water Ground Stone
Nihon: awase-kagami no okurimono
The Nine Seas and the Eight Mountains
Yureru kagami no yoake: Rocking Mirror Daybreak
(linked poems with Makoto Ōoka)
With the Water
Mooning
Playseeds
This Time This Place
Meditation Seeds

—Voiceweave Trilogy—
Muscle and Machine Dream (the '80s)
Morningdew (the '70s)
Downinside (the '60s)

—Translations & Remakings—
The Poetry and Poetics of Ancient Japan
A String Around Autumn
Devil's Wind: A Thousand Steps
The Ghazals of Ghalib:
(with W.S. Merwin, Adrienne Rich, William Stafford, et al.)

—Anthologies—
The New Poetry of Japan: the '70s & '80s
A Play of Mirrors: Eight Major Poets of Modern Japan
Japanese Poetry Now: 1945-1965

IRON HARP

BIRTH of the ONE-EYED BOY

Thomas Fitzsimmons

illustrations by
Karen H.-Fitzsimmons

La Alameda Press :: Albuquerque

Some of these poems, often in different form,
have been published in English or Japanese in:

Collections—
Yureru kagami no yoake: Rocking Mirror Daybreak
(Chikuma Shobo, Tokyo, 1983),
Nihon: awase-kagami no okurimono
(Iwanami Shoten, Tokyo, 1986),
Sextet: Six Powerful American Voices,
"The Dream Machine",
(Pennywhistle Press, Santa Fe, 1996*)*

Voiceweave Scripts—
Downinside and *Morningdew.*
Anthologies—
The Abraxas/5 Anthology, XY Files,
and *The Practice of Peace*

Periodicals—
ARX, Black Mountain Review, The Bridge, Choice,
East West Annual, imagesformedia.com, Kokubunkaku,
Kyoto Journal, Mobius, Nimrod, Passager, Plucked Chicken,
Poetry Kanto, poetrymagazine.com, Shincho,
Vision International, Wisconsin Review, and *Yefief*

ISBN :: 1-888809-19-1
Library of Congress # :: 99-73745

La Alameda Press
9636 Guadalupe Trail NW
Albuquerque, New Mexico 87114

For Karen

The situation of our time
surrounds us like a baffling crime

W. H. Auden
"New Year Letter" (1940)

CONTENTS

Prologue

Rainbow

When I was a kid playing hooky
spending my dime on a loaf of Greek bread
to eat dry
high on a hillside outside Lowell, Massachusetts
I did not think that I
would be sitting on Parnassus slope
high above Delphi
eating my loaf of Greek bread,
with feta, black olives, & retsina,
looking down through temple, valley, and time
to when I was a kid playing hooky
eating my bread dry
high on the hills above the Merrimack river
outside Lowell, Massachusetts.

Earth

M'mêre and City Hall

His maternal grandmother, *m'mêre*, in the bent
French that was all they spoke at home,
introduced him to corruption when he
was barely eight. Before that she taught him
to prowl for and prize dry twigs
and wood scraps, cardboard, old newspaper
to feed the black iron stove hunched
hungry in their tenement kitchen. By eight
he was ready for bigger things.

Locked in an old black dress, thin-faced tiny
m'mêre rocked out complaints, dark prophesies
about her back, him, his beautiful scared
young mother, Irene, who'd married an Irish
drunk, and of course had had to run.

While Irene did time in the Lowell mills
of the Yankee gods, *m'mêre*, dry, hurting,
and needed, rocked him out to school and back,
until after a fall one wet day she never went out
again; just rocked and balked. His job, his first,
was to fetch the medicine for her pain,
available to the poor at lower cost
if the poor got hold of a paper signed
by one of the rednosed Irish gents at City Hall,
hub of that most reasonable wheeling deal—

to get you've got to give. For people poor
enough the price was low: humiliation, and
one lousy pack of smokes. Eight is an age
of burgeoning pride and a pack was more
than he could buy so with joy he stole them
on his way to City Hall each time, absorbing
thereby a lesson in Civics, and learning to
always connect, as the storyteller says, "only connect."
And to keep the chin tucked well in while whistling
as though you've always known everything:

kindling and scraps that have kept him warm
all through these years of writing and talking
far from the old black stove, the delphic drone
of *m'mère* holding hard to the rock
of a creaking chair.

Dad

Big hands hoisting him   plunk
onto a bar next to big plates
bigfaces bigvoices bigfingers
poking him eat—eat! Big

fists pounding his mother bent
covering her face whimpering
cornered by the stove.

That night they run away run
from New Jersey and her job
to Lowell and her mother.

Only once more: KNOCK! KNOCK!
on the kitchen door, years later, back of
their tenement, end of the alley;
Irene opens, reels back shrieking
blood flooding her face—
curses and a manshape big.

He grabs the knife beside his plate
runs lunges stabs stumbles his
head explodes he bounces on the floor—
more curses big feet clumping
fading gone.

Your father! She aims it through
blood and broken teeth straight
into the center of his head
tattooing a rose of hatred there
scarlet   white   and pure as bone.

Mom

His mother abandoned him when he was 10,
put him in an orphanage—tricked him there—
so she could work and they could eat and he
wouldn't be on the streets: chain of reasoning
meaningless to him, child chained in needs

of his own. Thirty years later advised by state-
certificated analytical incompetents tricked out
in uniformly clear career-reason-wrap he tricked *her*
into a nut-house, and left her there, abandoned.

He ran away from the orphanage of course
and managed just fine on the streets. And came
to realize his mother's ways did not qualify her,
except as staff, for residence in that zoo.
So she got out, too. —And then . . .

And then.

Prayer

Tall in his bloodline the streetfighter struts—
and it's time to dance to that tune again
oldest of runes seared on his heart, sung
in his blood, stunned in his bones. Song
red as the sun dying.

As He must.
As I must not.

O father let me leave your rage unsung
as the thorns reaped in Bethlehem
the wines burned in Paris, the hymns
that never reach lip—

let the white birds sing the sea change
from terror to dawn.

Water

His mother reels
inside his brain, his father
snakes into his liver;
he kneels by cloud–veined water
to hear   to heal   his name.

Leaving His Old Mother
Slowly Going Mad

torn clouds—
gold leaves cling against
   west wind

dawn seep
of ice blue light—gulls
   cry him awake

   alone
 he memorizes
the rain

While the Sea Runs

while the sea runs
the years grow

and the heart

the years go
wherever the years go

the heart holds
however it can

none of it is easy

all of it
is all there is

no more

Fire & Water

Colors in the Heart

1
The Bay of Angels

His grandmother, resurrected, sits in black
at a time-green steel-vine-crusted cash machine
in the hardware store of a village in the Maritime Alps
just north of Cannes and west of the Bay of Angels.

He goes in there every day or two to look
at her, peer over shelves of everycolor
bric-a-brac at the thin white knife of a face
he carries carved inside his own
and never thought to see again
with its twisted chip of an almost smile coiled
in the center of a sigh that's kept her all
through the years hungry as a child.

Today that same thin never-rising voice
plucks at an iron harp of everyday miseries
for another woman old as herself who wants
to listen wants to run is caught in a resonance
riddled and dear as Leda's with
her hissing Swan.

2
The Edge

The Romans cut the trees here into ships
for trade and war. The oak, all the tough,
hard stuff, is gone, and every summer
the new pines burst, burn to the mistral
wind that whips in from the Alps.

Northward the ridges twist and fold and
climb until high in the Alps there are
no trees at all. Whole villages are built
of stone so unrelentingly gray that from
above the houses seem the gathered shards
of shattered mountain bones.
                                             Each village
holds one stonecold cavedark church where
Mary, the only bright thing there, stands
in blue and white, hands open, chest open,
heart scarlet in the cold cold dark.

The dawn there explodes in silence, flows
out along the frozen sea of towered
crumbling alpine ridges clear to the Danube,
and down the spine of Italy.
                                        From Cannes,
Roman anchor for its road to Spain, you can
take the train now all the way back to Rome,
and further—down to the rotting bones and barges
on the blood beaches of Salerno, Naples, Anzio

and down to the water's edge, where memory flowers
green and phosphorescent—gangrene bubbling
in the heart.

The Beach at Anzio, Italy, 1944

sunset
eats itself
black

sunrise
has us
raw

The Beaches After 1945

Blood still crusts the water—
music dries into a round
of rusted names:
palm to severed palm, ground
to final, tidal, membrane.

Mind can't unwind
that tide—heart drowns in
that twist of slaughter/
laughter where Kali, bleeding,
cradled us in her thighs.

Rocking Mirror

In this clear water he sees
his face
as in the sea long years ago
rocking among the bodies
of friends, bits and pieces
of bodies of friends, not
friends—who knows, how know
which hand is a friend's when
no arm, shoulder, face
completes the hand? How
know how to look so's not
to bleed into your own brain,
scream again, gag the salt the oil
the blood that streaks the sea the raft
your eyes?

How forget the one face,
yours, rocking on the fire,
bobbing in a mirror
of human garbage?

Flame and oil face streaked
with memories held cold now
in clear blue water.

Birth of the One-Eyed Boy

1. No!

the ship dead
his friends around him dying on a raft
again

slips back into the dark
the quiet cool
dark inside . . .

. . . back out
into the roaring sun
the pain eating his mind away
eating his body
the pain that is his body
is him

the terror
the horror
the stink

one dead at least
shit and piss
flesh beginning to rot

. . . out so long?
himself dead too?

away again
into the cool quiet
sacred black

out again . . .
nothing changed

except the stink
worse now

all that's left of them
his friends
their strength

a smell

no wind
swelling white-tipped water
sun . . . sky . . . sea . . .
nothing

a sea of fire when he clutched the raft
burning oil everywhere
ships blazing screams up close
guns planes depth-charges
noise noise noise

now
nothing—
going to die
this time

this time no help

this time   dead

will not damn it die in this stink

moves to . . .
no . . .
not moving . . .
can't move!

will move!
will not die like this

Move!

claws at the space between the slats
drags across inches miles of fouled wood
gets there

next to them
inside the stink
wrapped in it

over
get them over

twists   hauls . . .
with a last burst
rises up over one of the bodies
strains to lift . . .push . . .
roll it into the sea . . .

collapses

face down
into liquefying flesh

screams

tries to scream
gags

fades away again
back into the black

slowly this time
slow enough to know just how
it will be with him

rotting
face down
on a rotting friend

2. Yes !

what . . . ?
a hospital
another hospital

on his back
in a hospital
again

without memory
again

then memory

and
heat
terror
rage

tearing at the straps holding
him to the bed

not be held
will not be held
never again

is surrounded

too much they whisper
too much too young too often

he's snapped

only normal
poor thing

he is not
he snarls
a poor thing
and none of it
NONE OF IT
is normal!

•

then the colonel
just coming by to visit

then a major
then another

too much rank
what . . . ?
one after another
they come just to visit just to suggest
that maybe they can help him
help him feel better
maybe help him get even
with the bastards
who again and again have killed his friends
and left him and them to die
rot on the water

merchant seamen
with never a weapon
no way to fight back

would he like a weapon?

they can give him weapons
weapons and training

a chance to fight back

good for him to fight back
burn off the rage
before he burns out

weapons . . . training
pistol garrote knife
tracking camouflage signaling

and
when it's over
an honorable out
maybe a medal
confidential
of course
and something for later
when he grows up

screw your medals
your growing up

in and out
the black the light
the silence the voices
out and in

then
like catching fire
he gets it

no longer cares about the rank
pressed uniforms
buttery tones

listens now
very carefully

agents have been left along the coasts of southern Italy
to spot convoys call in the U–boats call in the planes that
in minutes reduce ships and their crews to the burning
hulks shards of flesh he knows so well then shell and strafe
lifeboat and raft leave whatever flesh survives to slowly
roast in salt and sun

these bastards must be tracked down
found and destroyed
eliminated
like animals

one by one
found and made to disappear
without explanation

no trace
no remains

each disappearance
a seed of terror
among them
they'll wonder
never be sure
if they are betrayed
who's betrayed them

forming small units right now
they croon
secret
have to move fast
elimination units
ambush
not assassination
not murder
ambush
old honorable
war tactic
guerrilla tactic

can he
they are asking
will he

kill

up close
with his hands?

up close
and quiet . . .

and from the quiet inside himself
he hears himself
say it clearly—

Yes

Yes!

The One-Eyed Boy Dreams

The hills are there
                              still

brown shriveled hills
brown wrinkled water

later when I had lost the hate when
I had gained that loss they
would litany me names of friends
mates I'd seen drown scream burn
crying like babies
count me the ships lost
to agents like him
count me my days in boats on rafts
my ravings in hospitals
where I'd first said yes
to this hell
yes

turned wolf by dogs whining
somebody has to   somebody
had to

                              very still

and the monastery
with its cross

and the old stone pile
broken shepherd's hut

                              very still

half a mile of dry mean twisted brush
crackling in any wind at any touch
hell to slip through at night

Hey lobo, how's your belly?
Have you eaten   lobo? Eat.
Eat meat.

all day we watched the hills
slipped through the lines at dark
slipped the river on logs
four boys four hates four stinking logs
a crusted land   very still

and *he* was
as arranged
there

in the broken shepherd's shelter
hunched
watching the river trail

I kept the glasses on him a full
five minutes from thirty feet
          we were that quiet   lobo

seeing just how he was
just how he would likely move

Quietly   lobo.
Do you smell it now   lobo?
Above all do not hurry.

then handed off the glasses
unsheathed the knife
moved out
circling
while they went straight uptrail
as expected as arranged
whispering the expected whisper
that would ease him

I saw his shoulders loosen

Yes   lobo. Quietly.
The belly low but not dragging.
No sound—Care. Rhythm.
Patience.

with a knife always
it is hard   and it stays
in the hand   in the fingers
years don't change it

I let them drag him to the river

he had to disappear
his buddies had to wonder
but I helped with the rocks the rope
the sack

after we slid him into the water
fast star-filled water, Jimmy
younger, thinking he hated more,
was sick   then ashamed

       Eat   lobo.
       Smell the wet red smell.
       Smell the bones—inside the bones
       such sweetness.

Crack Up

when his hands died
he screamed

and his face cracked
flaking here and there black
among the gray crusted cinders
of the way he had chosen

the trees shuddered
as dead his fingers
were hammered into place
each nailing one white bird

—he is
beasted
gored

bleeds worms
his soul is slime

bury him
let the salt wind
raze   let
the tides take him

the crabs
eat him clean

Rest & Recreation, Capri 1945

beyond the window an olive
old as Naples sings and nods
to a man hung rotting from
its highest limb—

a long black song it
summons white screeching
birds to drink the eyes
pick the bones

The One-Eyed Boy Dreams
Nails & Crosses

Dream wanderers in the morning
of the world, naming the first things,
weaving the songlines

      the mothers, they say, are weeping
      tonight; the mothers rock & weep;
      the place is Dresden

In Toledo a one-armed man makes swords;
how he lost his arm is a secret
from us, from him

      The time is noon

From his balcony hawks seem to fill the valley;
thin cries of greed, the velvet rub of wings
against burnt air

      crisp air of Moorish Spain
      caked blood of Christ

The nail was a primal invention, a joining
of mind and matter; a dream whose time came early
the place was near a forest
the sun was late afternoon, just before
eventide cool, and the next dream,
the hammer

the mothers, they say, are weeping
tonight; the mothers rock & weep;
the place is Hiroshima

nailing the dawn.

Air

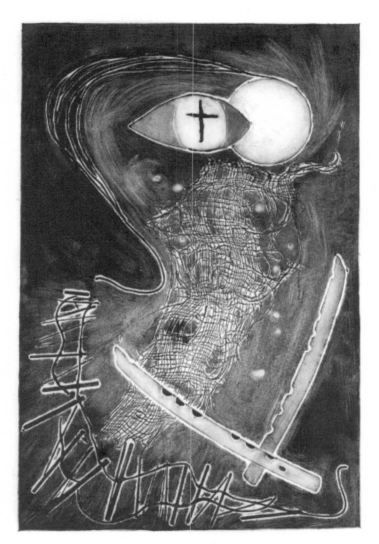

The One-Eyed Boy Remembers Zero

He remembers Christ the son
how he came down off his cross
and carried it to the highest hill
for miles around—it was

a clear day and you could see
could even hear just how much
trouble it would all come to
all that carrying on about who
was who: who the son who the father
who the ghost who entered Mary—

remembers how the heavens came down
to stare stayed to wonder and the old
stars ran here and there keening trying, while
the old gods died, to find themselves in the new
heavenly score—*anno domine*—and the years
wound back down to zero—remembers

how after 20 more centuries of goodly
killing and his own hands bloody and
his star burning down to zero she came
down off a higher hill to walk with him
in a place where no stars ran nor hummed
a withered time-rotted sunless plain under high
crusted red dry ridges cracked like teeth like
the scorched bones left when soul's fire runs down
to leap into the blind sunset cross of faith.

She had no tongue for cross-wise words
no need to tally wounds—moved with him
into a story where no gods birth or die
where one woman one man love.

The One-Eyed Boy
Contemplates Salvation

The sun burns down again,
night nets a haze of flames:
stars to feed his spine's dim
ritual dreams of Venus Mars
salt bread fire.

In the fire he spins as the wind rages
whispers
folds him for a moment incandescent
between making and unmaking
pure.

•

And the sea is new again
brings to the ship's high steel sides
moon-riddled legends of the lands
on either side—Troy burning
Homer staring Rome sacked
Jerusalem stunned.

Long flames along a planet's turnings.

Star dust spins in his fingers
sun syllables cascade in his tongue
 —lift him out of time   then fade
like moonlight   flesh after drowning.

•

If under a moon pale as his own blind eye
he had found a way back to the cathedral
could he have spun that legend into his own
bone & blood?

There is haze in the woods now
spring buds?   more fire?
The one-eyed boy cannot decide.
With wind and reed he hums
whistles spells to grow another eye.

He Questions the Mirror

Not in the knife
     and not
he thinks
     in the gun
not even in the twist
of stretched silk sinew
     but maybe
in the air around
or the time around that
     or the black
back behind the glass
     the black that
makes the mirror mirror
maybe there

if not there then
in the shells spun like pearls
around seed
the lights wound into signs
or that raw wound winding
through the world

AGAPE

opening like that—
blurred image of a future effect
held in the wings
where everything that is

to be waits to be
called and named
and of course judged
worthy or not of
the name the calling
the wound
        the mirror

and all the while
time
        as we call that
tames the play
back behind the black

how else could we afford
or be afforded space
to blow our horns bind our wounds
trim our sails to winds that fill
what little heart there is and time
that's only just enough for you and me

and the other
the one who one day may
slice clean through time
scattering blade gun and cross
shattering memory
before it sings again
out of the dark round well
of the black-backed time-tilted
mirror
that always knows
your name.

He Considers Memory

Sanity is in forgetting . . .

(Truth is in the grains
one at a time
between two fingers coupled
and in the rain before it freezes
and in the rain frozen
in the absence of rain
of grain of fire
in the stillness
of uncoupled fingers
in the old
in the wind
in the motionless silent clowns.)

 . . . and in the morningdew.

He Dreams Cathedrals

In cathedrals on the edge of day
blue engages green, tangles gold
to dancing flames of resonance;
stone filaments thread shadow into
glass, coil music to choired silence.

Cathedrals spring from clay.
The dream impales the dreamer.

Fencing the Sky

Boxed as symbol the rose the flame
are not rose and flame but signatures
mined for images intricate as the mix
of rage and grace we barter to gain
strength and measure, twist Other to
mirror, square our crooked circles
of blood-anchored stone.

•

Earth spins on this cross of lies
feeds space signed pieces of itself—
seeds void with meaning so we can
find it there again, cage it here again
in our brain-eating frenzies of faith
that suck dry the flow of artery and
vein feeding each believer's brain
heart's blood and rhythm—life's fleshy
only answer to the bland viciousness
of a soul surprised.

•

Whining for meaning we sour
the everywhere glistening sap,
fence the sky so's not to fall
into the all-around white, the well
of all our colors. Dizzy for truth

we drive it deep as sword will reach
and in a mix of delicacy and rut howl
for Shiva, Buddha, Christ, Mohammed,
Madonna, Elvis, whoozits

spent, fold
into the silence of a heron dreaming
blue archipelagos of stone eternal in
a sea burned white as sun bleached shell.

•

We weave reweave little magic nets to
catch the dazzling silver fish Belief
—memory babbling into its own eyes
under the swelling rain that lifts
the trees that give us sweetly back
the breath we daily squeeze into
promise, prayer, deceit.

•

Dying in the sun, foul in our nest of
cosmic straw, starseed, timedust,
we burn to see ourselves golden again
in the entrails of the universal ash.
Water tides all through us, through every
gate we lock, and air weds grace to power
with never any holding—we cast up monument,
doctrine, blame, barter grace for praise,
kill each other, whistle up a grave.

•

Nugget, gilt, or tinsel, our Truths turn
puzzle. Their ruins teach us music. The fish
in our eyes paint us poems. Our fences rot.

The sky takes us back.

The Hand

Black
      black
            black

so many kinds of black   even the stars.

It is dark
I am afraid of you

the wind freezes
the mind locks like a hand

perhaps we will endure
        bruised
        sky bruised
in the wild places

perhaps we will survive
in the shadows
until we can trust the sun again
perhaps we will eat the shadows
and be sustained.

Paint it black.

Black is the color of my true love's hair

black is not a color
is the absence of color
love is a color
absence a curse
curse of the flutes that will never be played.

We are all afraid
it is wise.

Time is a dance   time is a long crusted way

and the bones hand-made along the way
sliver into our souls our hearts
the brain's fat hoard of needs and reasons
in the skull's moist locked little cave.

I would unlock you
with these hands I would spin to cover you cloth
blazing with brightcolor

but the crows curse and clack
the flaring flesh oozes black

soon even the grass will bleed
into the wind's long hands
gathering stones gathering bones
and we will all weep
but the wind will not be filled

not by the rank wells of our eyes
the bloody stubs of our fingers

there is blood in tongues
blood dancing end/beginning
there is blood but we are cold

the dark prowls our veins.

We cannot rise and dance
and if we try to rise merely
it is not permitted.

Let it all then be as it must be
we will dance without rising dance
in absolute stillness spin with fear
and stone gracefully into the air

puzzled   mocked   winged   airy

until terror is of last night
today there is breath after breath
eye open   eye closing   eyelash
poised against sun   grass in the nostril
air on the tongue   and a hand
sweet on the belly

the hand is the dancer speaking
the hand is the star brought here
the hand is the moon articulate
the hand is the man winging
the woman knowing   their hands
meeting   placing something into
carefully   nothing

that we—
who carved the first flute
and blew into it
and behold
the very air was charmed
—might have light to eat.

dawn—

temple bell

hum

Epilogue

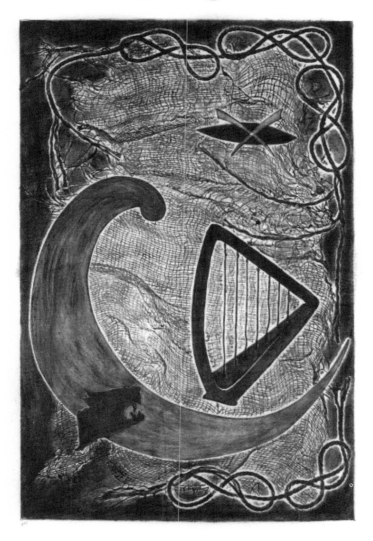

Menton:
Another Perfect Day in Paradise

Lounging on a balcony over the azure
meeting of France and Italy, finishing up

with 70 starting 71, having a birthday
by this sea where all the counting started,

waiting for a thought, insight, giggle,
something to mark the occasion, event,

achievement—but as numbers merely follow
precede others how make of that an occasion

for anything but a glance over
the shoulder a look up the road

to the next corner where if there is
anyone up-there back-there, was it

will it be you? The answer of course
soon will be no, but now it is yes—

you are, the chair is, water is the
blue of ages, and the sun's warmth

mixes with seawind's cool on your skin
under palm frond and passing cloud and

the mountains still shoulder down to a shore
where the Roman temples are no longer.

COLOPHON

Set in Monotype **Ehrhardt**,
based on the designs of Miklôs Kis, master
Hungarian punchcutter working in Amsterdam
during the late 1600's. Oldstyle in the Dutch
tradition, its narrow width and stubby serifs
create a dark tonality of dense character.

•

Book design by J. Bryan

Thomas Fitzsimmons went into World War II as an underage merchant seaman just after Pearl Harbor and was discharged from the USAAF just after Hiroshima. He was born in Lowell, Massachusetts, October 1926.

Formerly writer/editor for *The New Republic* (Washington, DC) and feature writer for *The Asahi Daily News* (Tokyo, Japan), he is author, translator, or editor of more than 60 books, 32 of which currently are in print. At present he is editor of two book series from University of Hawai'i Press: "Asian Poetry in Translation: Japan," and "Reflections."

Emeritus Professor of Literature, Oakland University, he has received a number of honors, including three National Endowment for the Arts fellowships (poetry, translation, and belles lettres), and several Fulbrights to countries in Europe and Asia. In the mid-1970s he and Karen Hargreaves-Fitzsimmons did a 16-month, 18-nation poetry reading/performance/lecturing/workshop tour through the Pacific, South Asia, the Middle East, and Europe under the auspices of USIS. They live just south of Santa Fe, where they publish Katydid Books, distributed by University of Hawai'i Press.

Fitzsimmons' *Planet Forces*, commissioned by 20th Century Unlimited and scored for soprano and 18 instruments by Peter Michaelides, had its premier December 12, 1998 in Santa Fe. A violin duo, composed by Toru Takemitsu to Fitzsimmons' and Makoto Ōoka's linked poems in the Japanese-English volume *Rocking Mirror Daybreak*, was commissioned by and is in the repertoire of New York's Lincoln Center Chamber Music Society. Other works by Toru Takemitsu and Makoto Ōoka to which he has contributed: *A Way A Lone*, and *From Far Beyond Chrysanthemums and November Fog*, chamber music; *From Me Flows What You Call Time*, Suite for Percussion and Orchestra; and the Symphony, *A String Around Autumn*.